GRAPHIC HISTORY

HARRIET TUBMAN
and the
UNDERGROUND RAILROAD

by Michael Martin

illustrated by Dave Hoover & Bill Anderson

Consultant:
Lois Brown, PhD
Museum of Afro-American History
Boston, Massachusetts

Capstone
press

Mankato, Minnesota

151 G ... 56002.

For information regarding permission, write to Capstone Press,
151 Good Counsel Drive, P.O. Box 669, Dept. R, Mankato, Minnesota 56002.
Printed in the United States of America

1 2 3 4 5 6 10 09 08 07 06 05

Library of Congress Cataloging-in-Publication Data
Martin, Michael, 1948–
    Harriet Tubman and the underground railroad / by Michael Martin; illustrated by
    Dave Hoover and Bill Anderson.
    p. cm.—(Graphic library. Graphic history)
    Includes bibliographical references and index.
    Audience: Grades 4–6.
    ISBN 0-7368-3829-5 (hardcover)
    ISBN 0-7368-5245-X (paperback)
    1. Tubman, Harriet, 1820?–1913—Juvenile literature. 2. Slaves—United States—Biography—
Juvenile literature. 3. African American women—Biography—Juvenile literature. 4. African
Americans—Biography—Juvenile literature. 5. Underground railroad—Juvenile literature. I. Title.
II. Series.
E444.T82M355 2005
973.7'115'092—dc22   2004015501

Summary: The story of Harriet Tubman and the Underground Railroad told in a
graphic-novel format.

Editor's note: Direct quotations from primary sources are indicated by a yellow background.

Direct quotations appear on the following pages:
Pages 9, 11, 13, 15, 16, 23, from *Harriet Tubman: The Moses of Her People* by Sarah Bradford
(Bedford, Mass.: Applewood Books, 1993).
Page 21, lyrics from "Steal Away to Jesus," an African American folk song, as quoted in
The Books of American Negro Spirituals compiled by James Weldon Johnson and
J. Rosamond Johnson (New York: Viking Press, 1940).
Page 27, from *Harriet Tubman* by Earl Conrad (Washington, D.C.: The Associated Publishers,
1943).

Art Director
Jason Knudson

Storyboard Artist
Keith Wilson

Colorist
Brent Schoonover

Editor
Donald Lemke

Acknowledgments
Capstone Press thanks Philip Charles
Crawford, Library Director, Essex High
School, Essex, Vermont, and columnist for
Knowledge Quest, for his assistance
in the preparation of this book.

Capstone Press thanks Dave Hoover and
Bill Anderson of Cavalier Graphics.

TABLE OF CONTENTS

Chapter 1
Growing Up a Slave

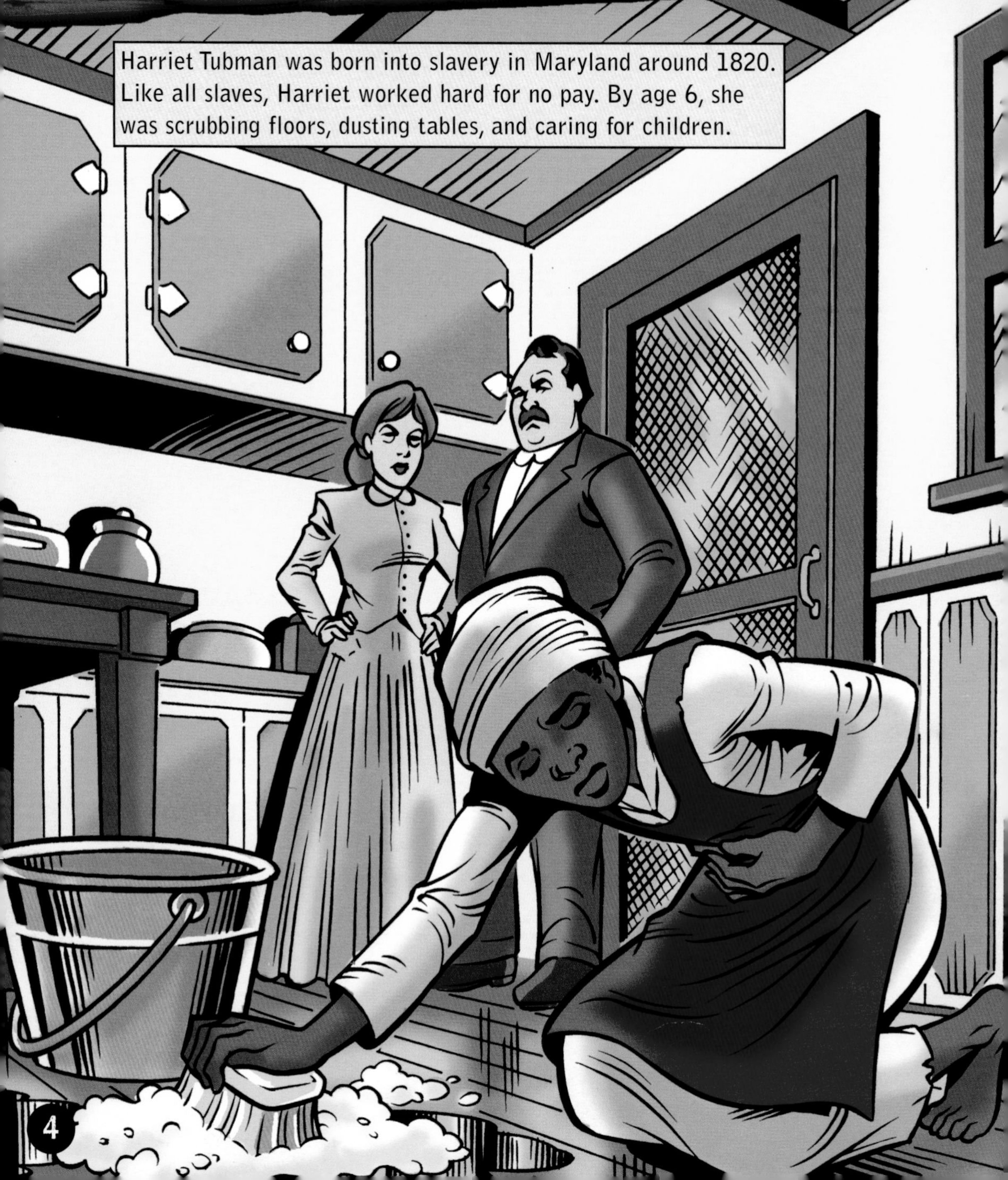
Harriet Tubman was born into slavery in Maryland around 1820. Like all slaves, Harriet worked hard for no pay. By age 6, she was scrubbing floors, dusting tables, and caring for children.

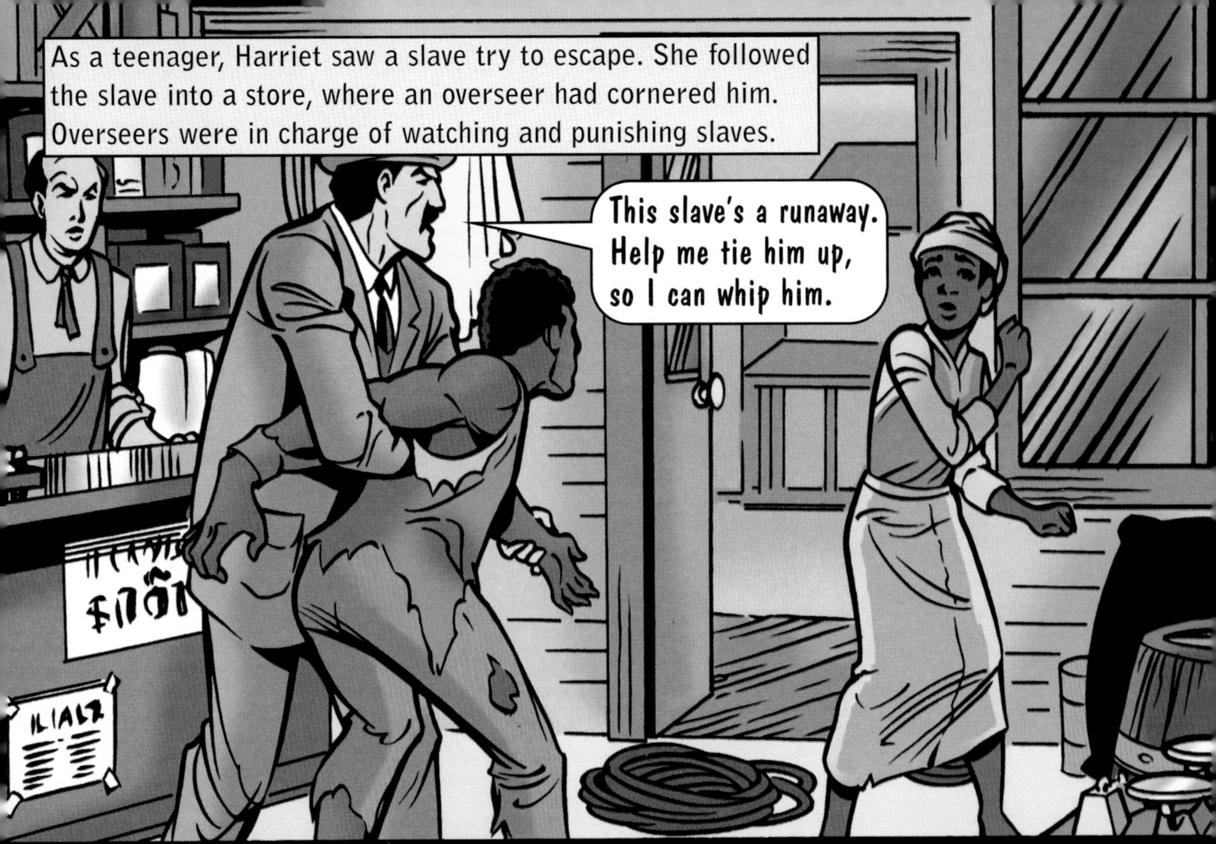
As a teenager, Harriet saw a slave try to escape. She followed the slave into a store, where an overseer had cornered him. Overseers were in charge of watching and punishing slaves.
This slave's a runaway. Help me tie him up, so I can whip him.

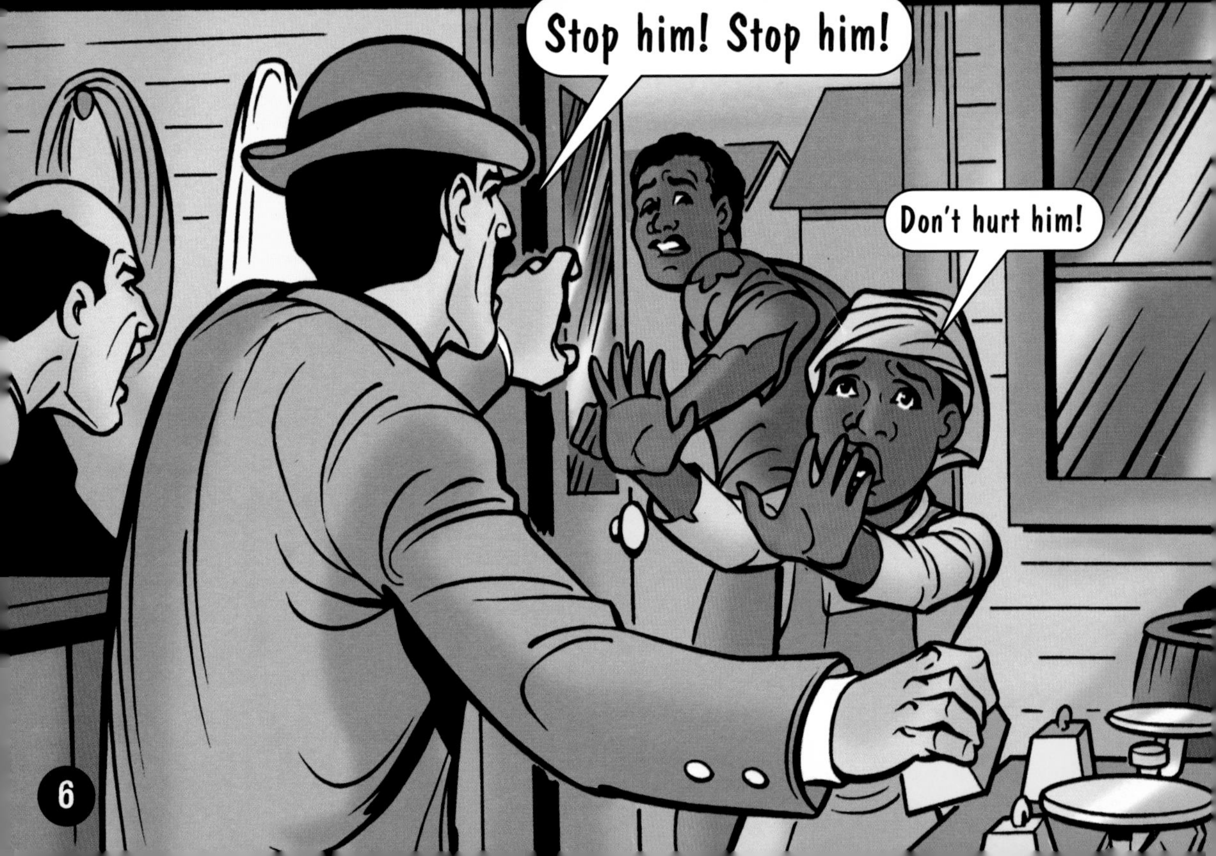
Stop him! Stop him!
Don't hurt him!

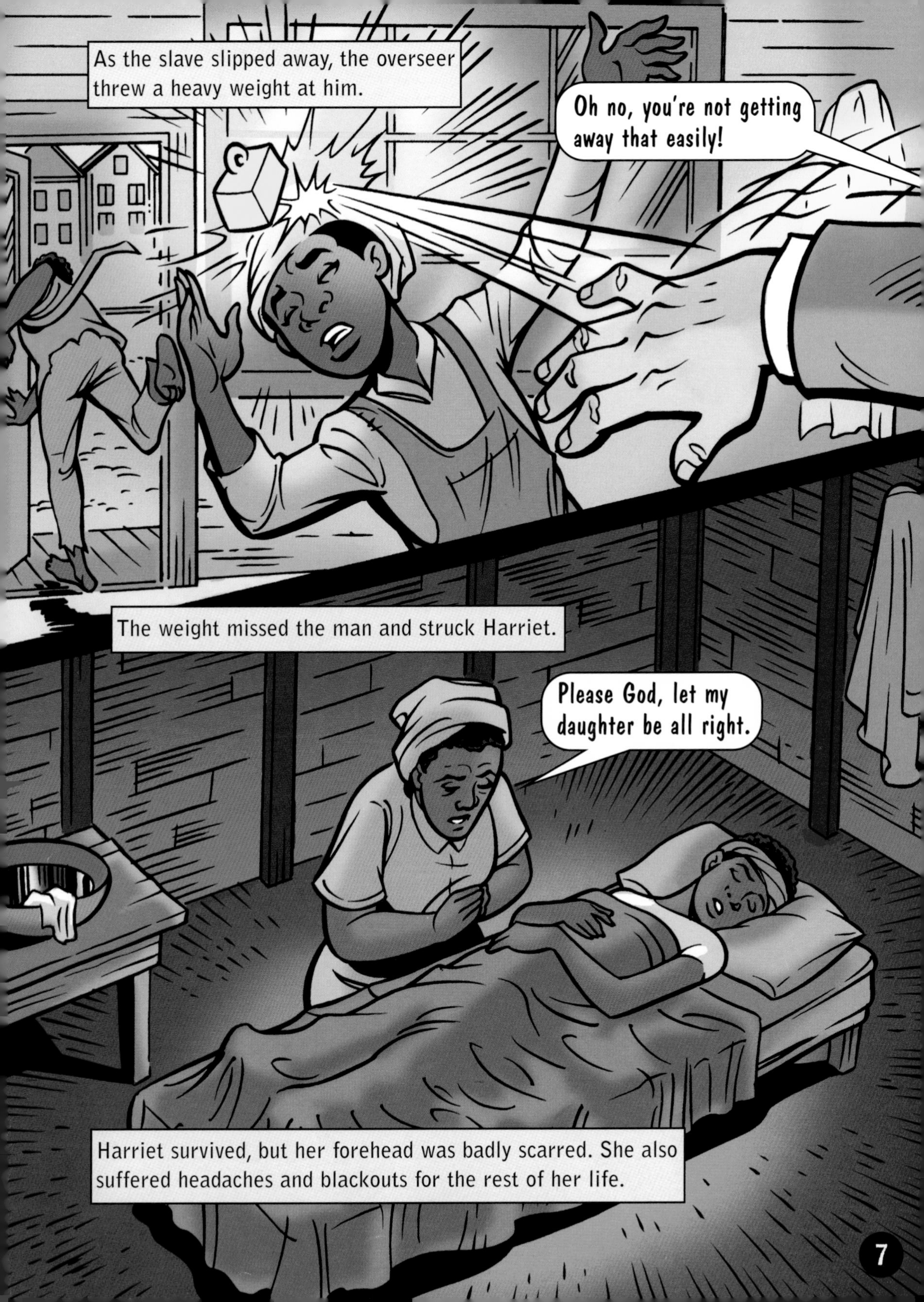

As the slave slipped away, the overseer threw a heavy weight at him.
Oh no, you're not getting away that easily!
The weight missed the man and struck Harriet.
Please God, let my daughter be all right.
Harriet survived, but her forehead was badly scarred. She also suffered headaches and blackouts for the rest of her life.

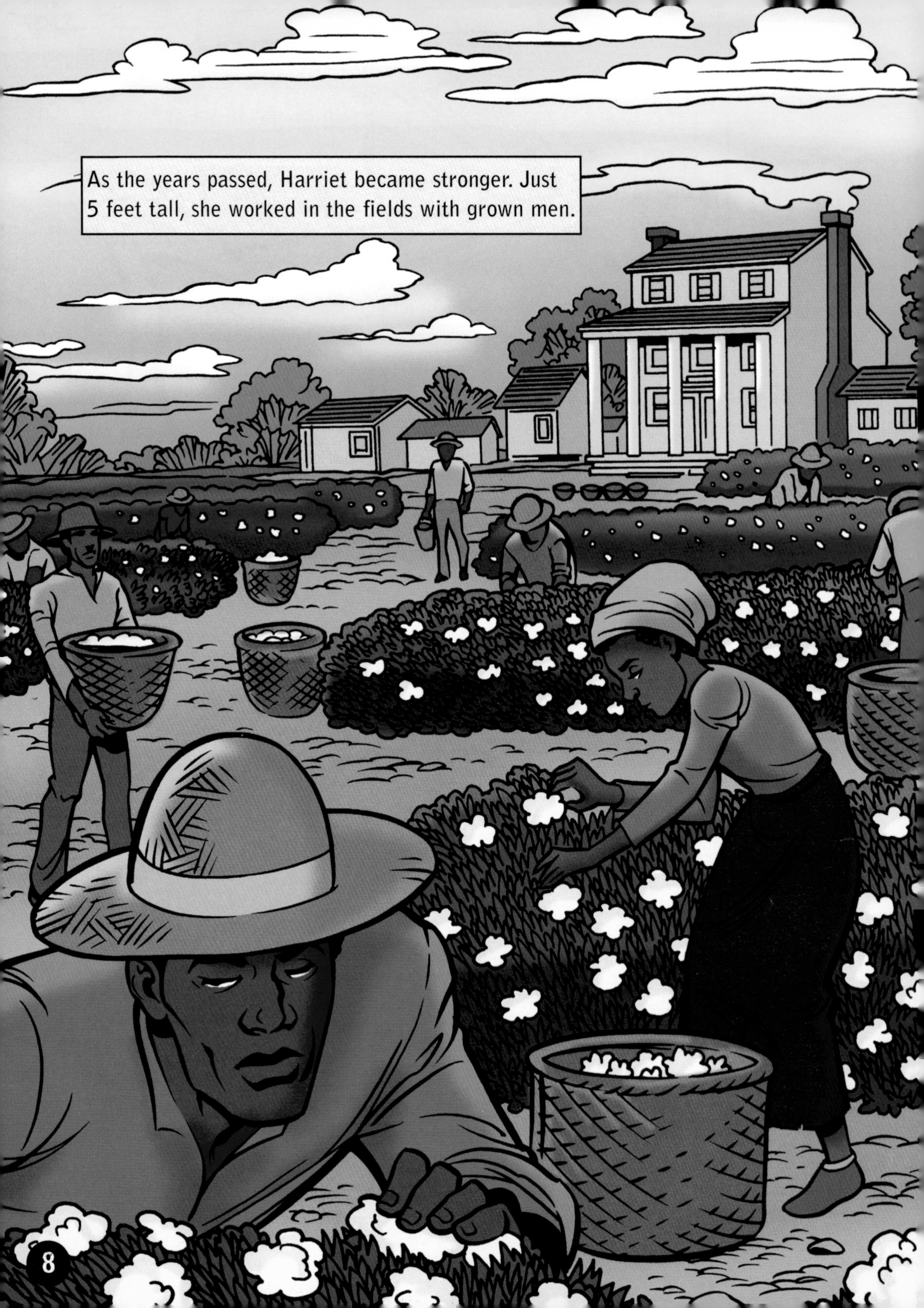
As the years passed, Harriet became stronger. Just 5 feet tall, she worked in the fields with grown men.

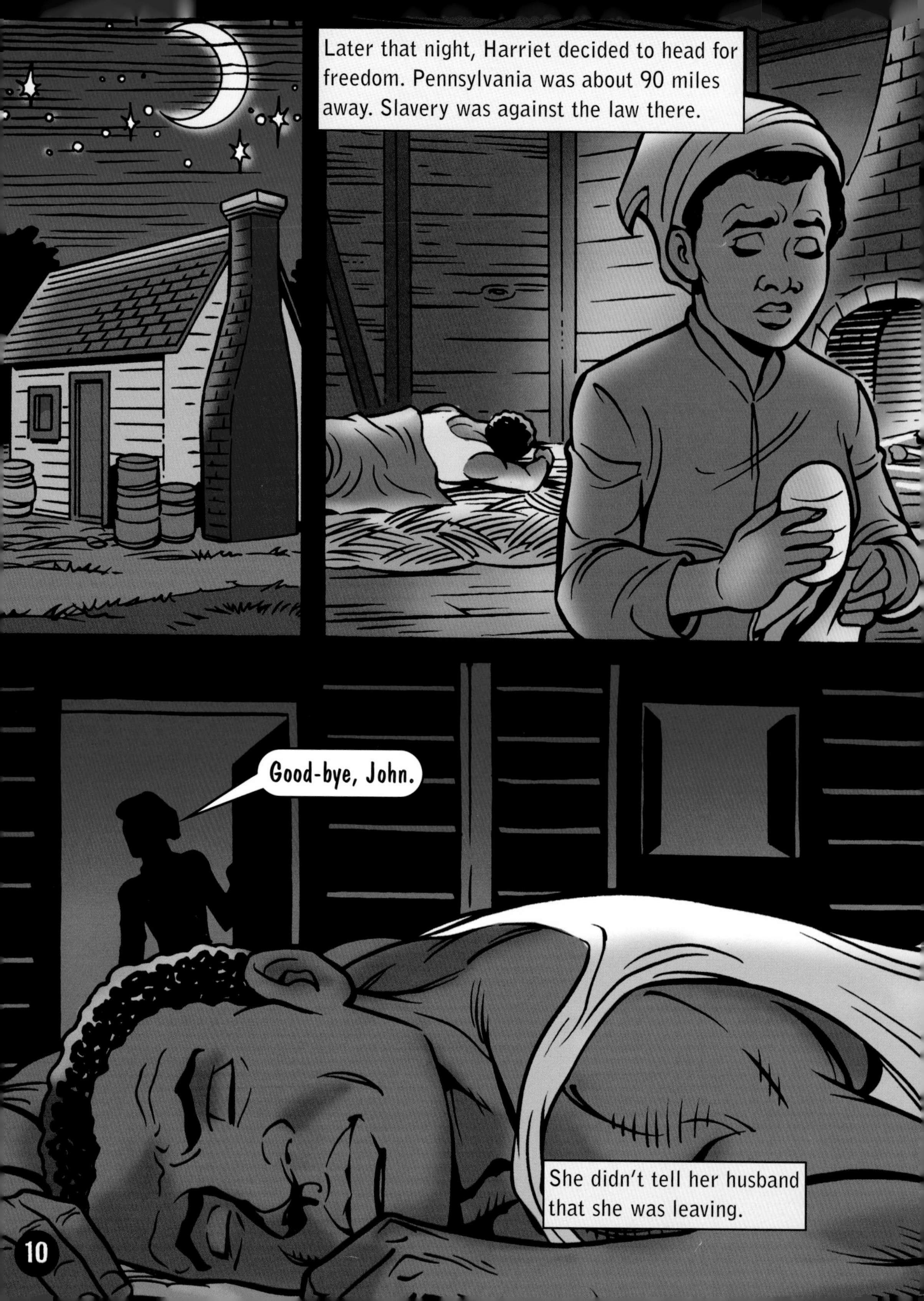
Later that night, Harriet decided to head for freedom. Pennsylvania was about 90 miles away. Slavery was against the law there.
Good-bye, John.
She didn't tell her husband that she was leaving.

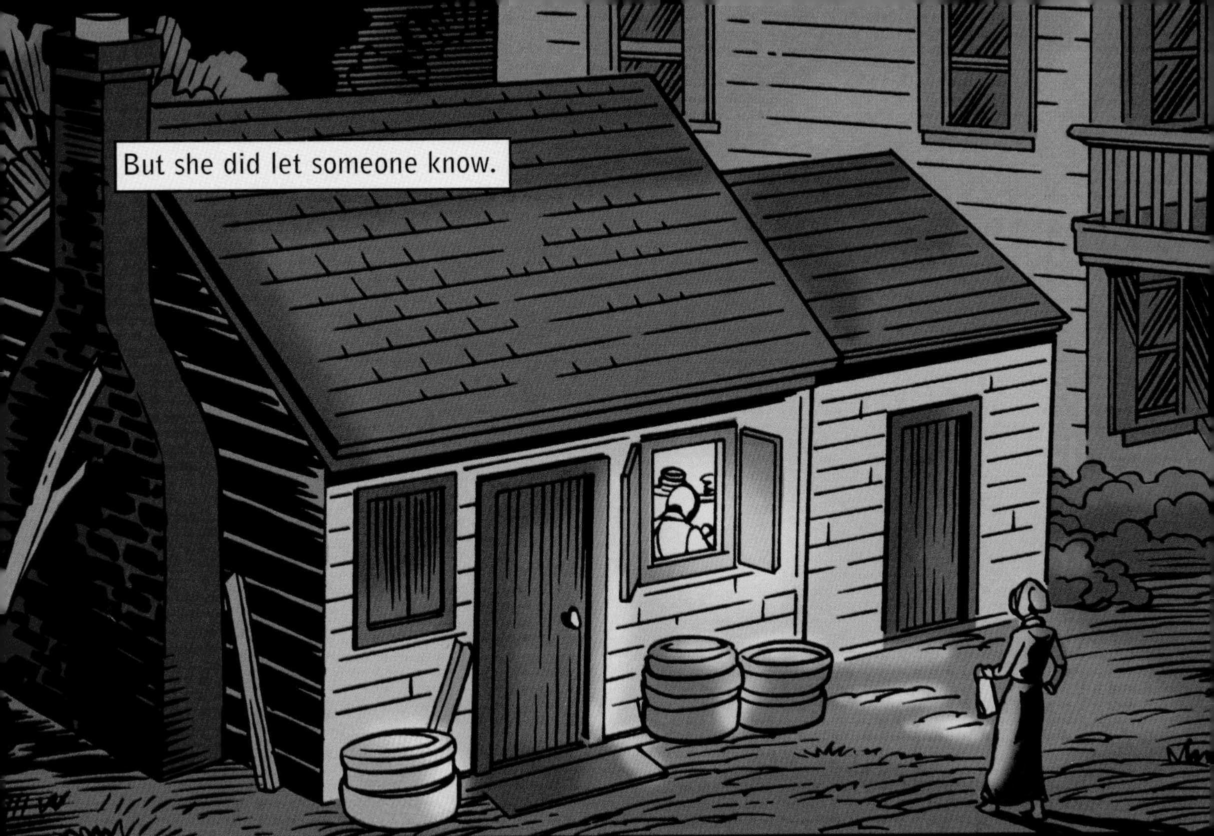
But she did let someone know.

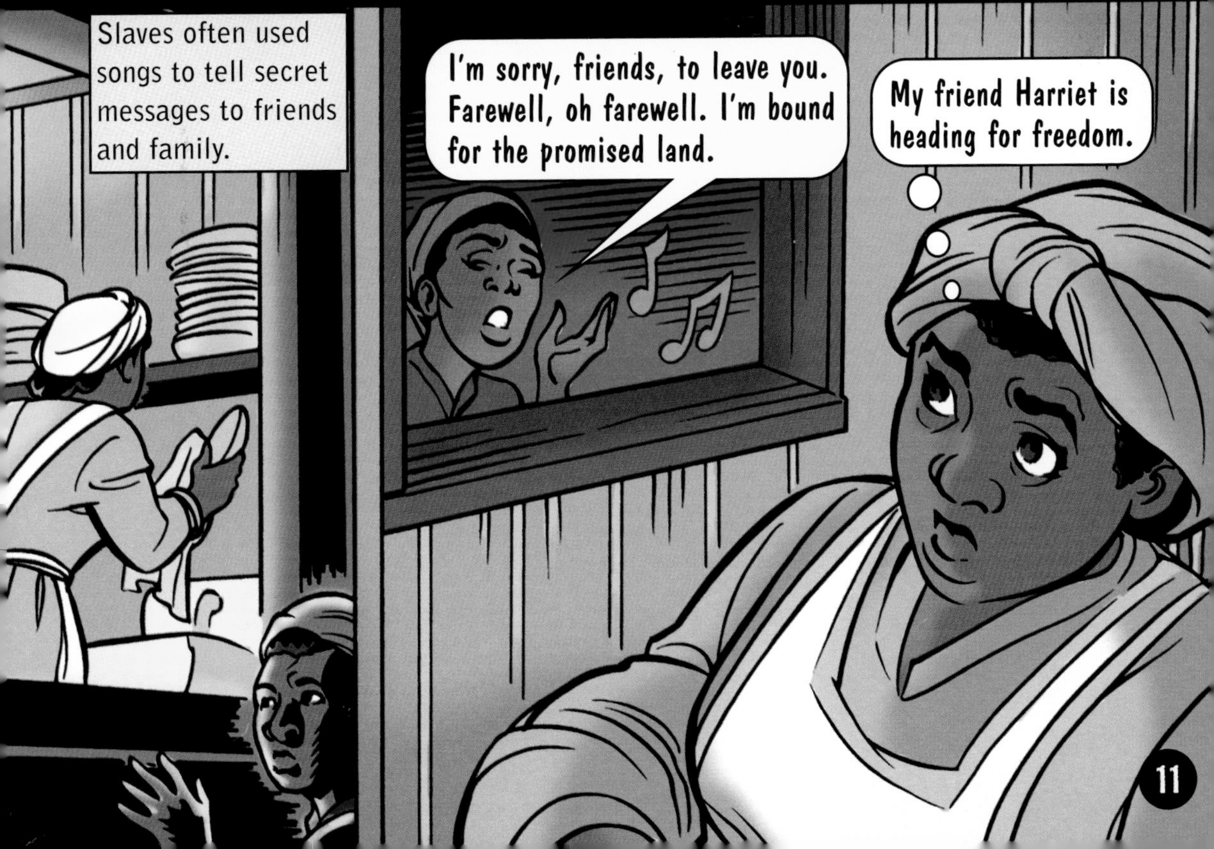
Slaves often used songs to tell secret messages to friends and family.
I'm sorry, friends, to leave you. Farewell, oh farewell. I'm bound for the promised land.
My friend Harriet is heading for freedom.

Chapter 2

Heading for the Promised Land

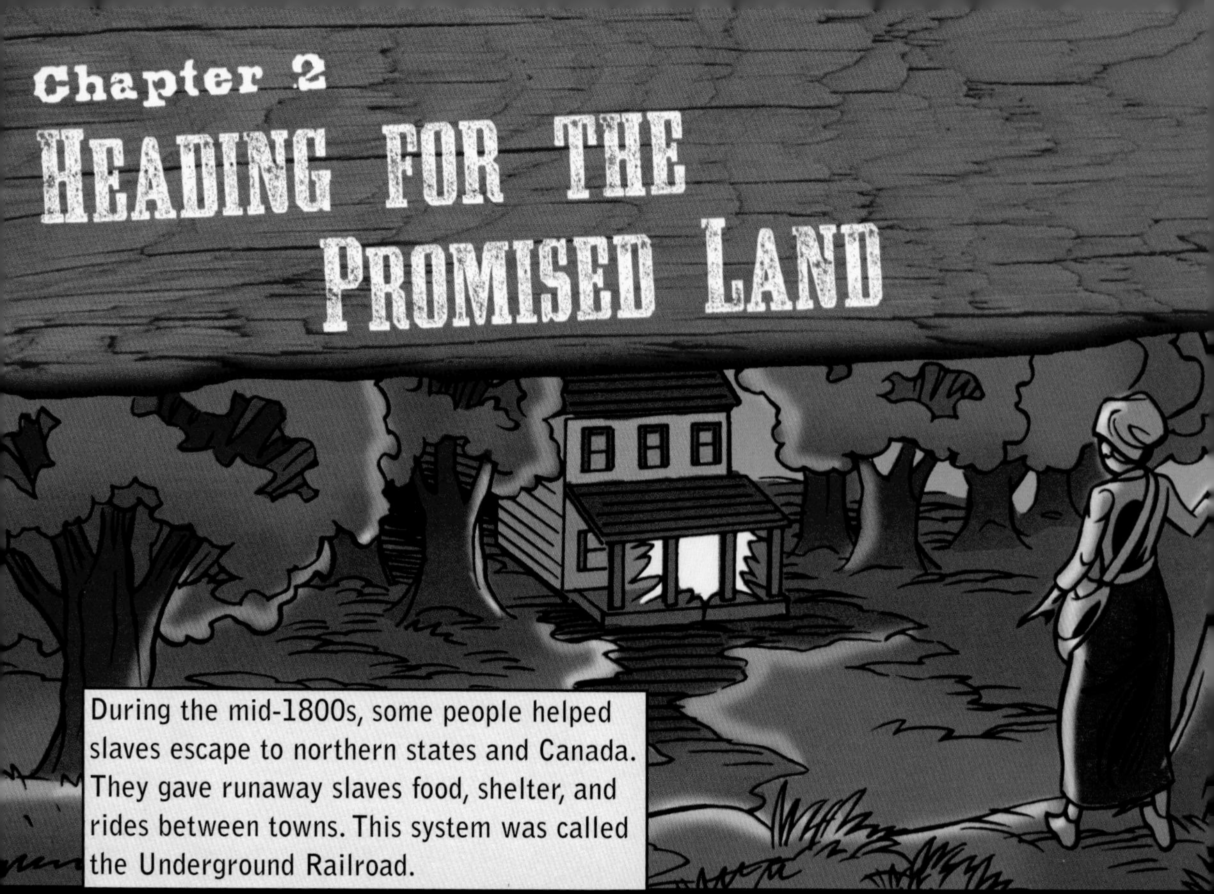
During the mid-1800s, some people helped slaves escape to northern states and Canada. They gave runaway slaves food, shelter, and rides between towns. This system was called the Underground Railroad.

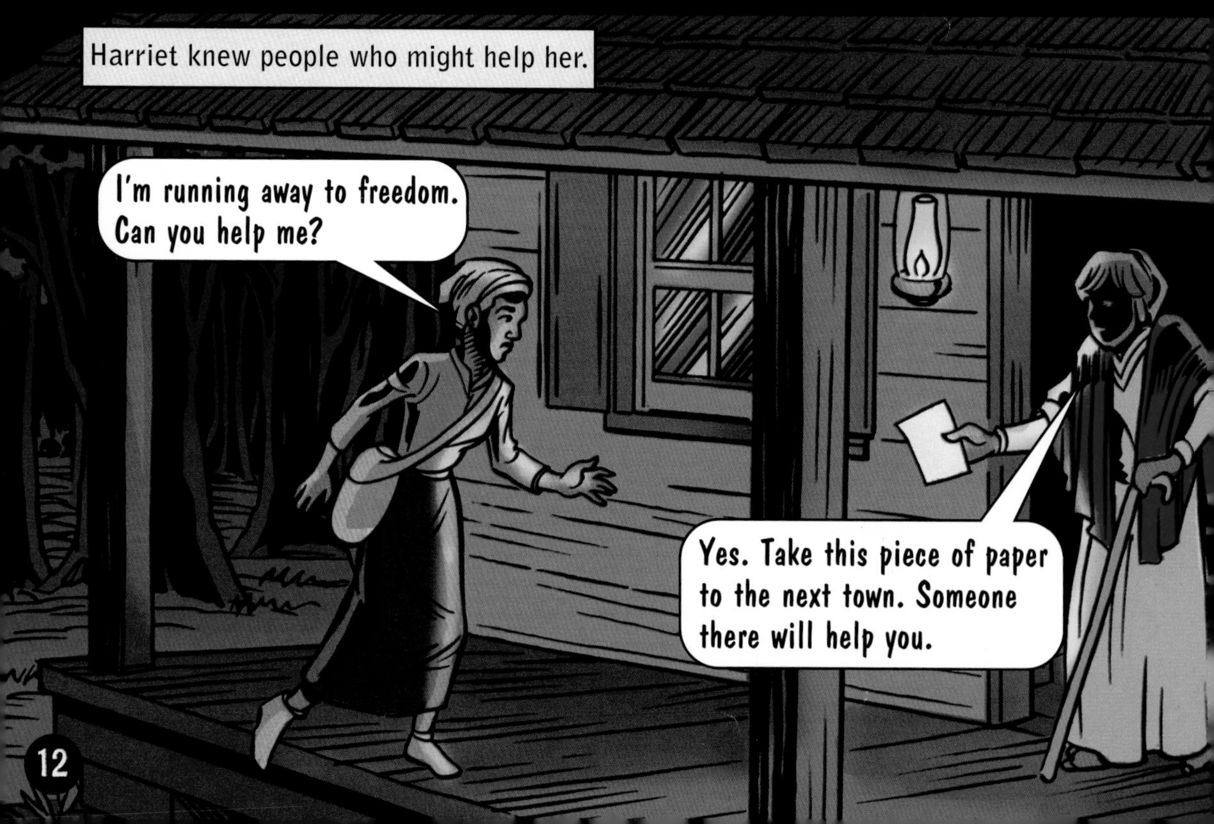
Harriet knew people who might help her.
I'm running away to freedom. Can you help me?
Yes. Take this piece of paper to the next town. Someone there will help you.

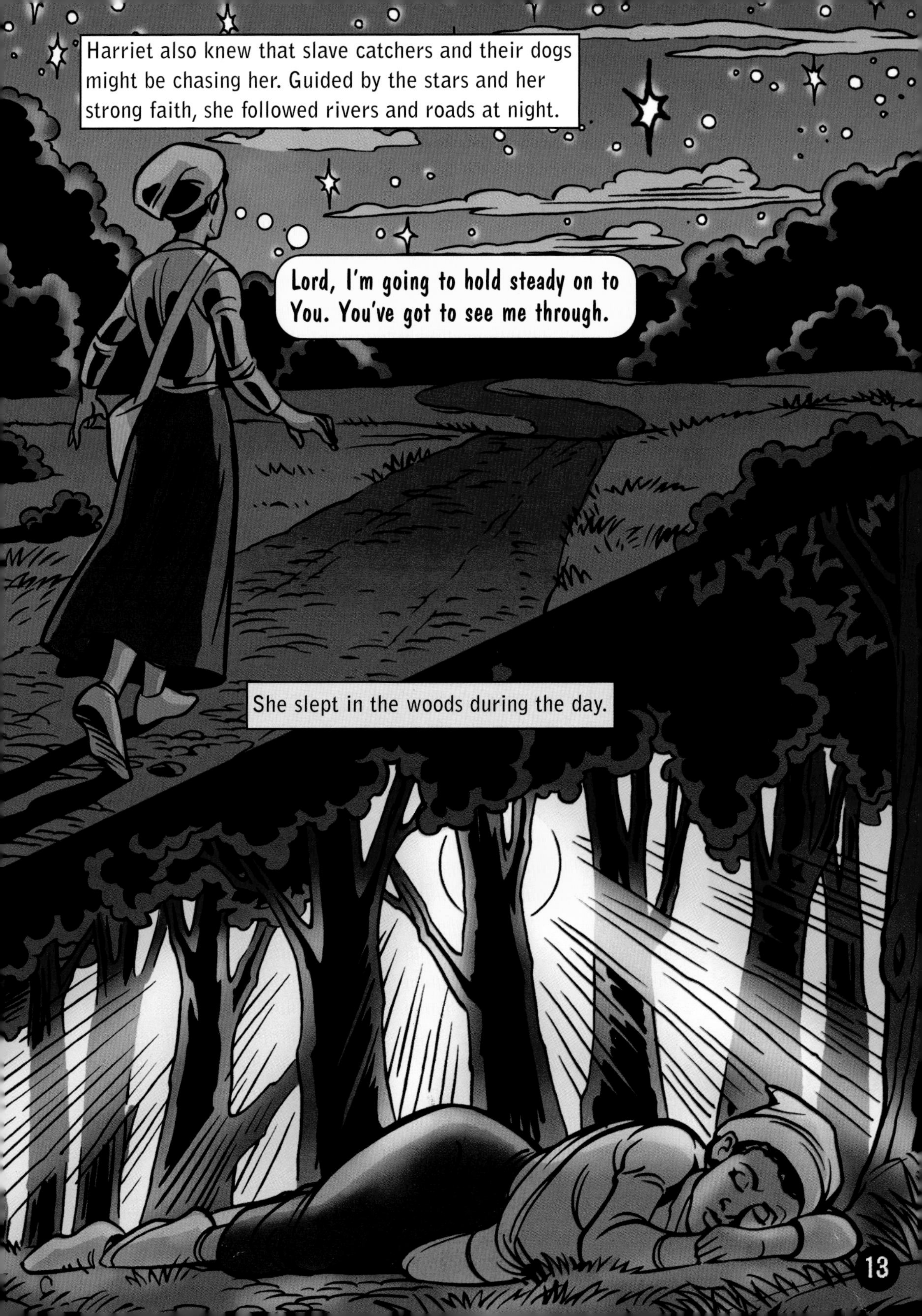
Harriet also knew that slave catchers and their dogs might be chasing her. Guided by the stars and her strong faith, she followed rivers and roads at night.
Lord, I'm going to hold steady on to You. You've got to see me through.
She slept in the woods during the day.

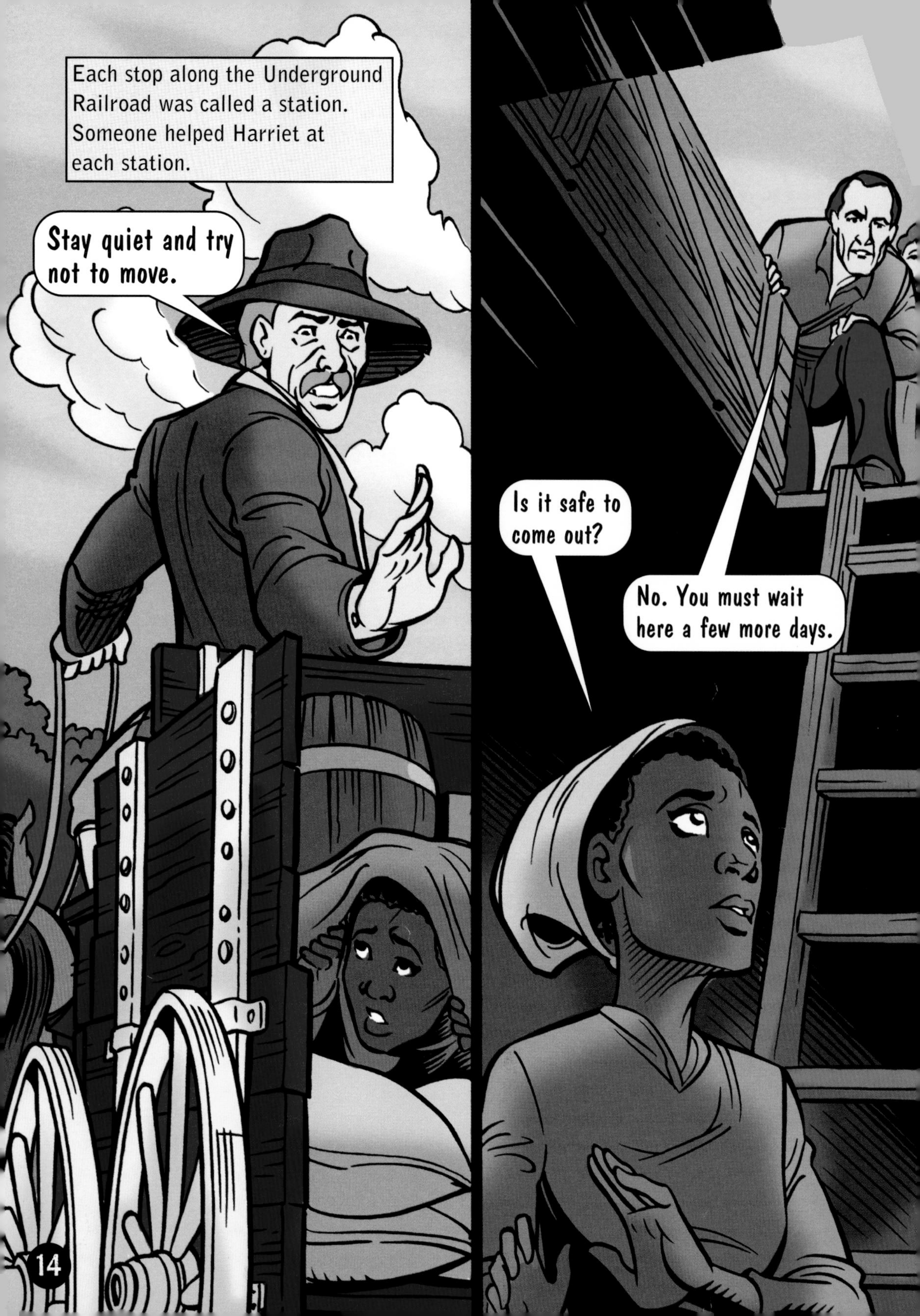
Each stop along the Underground Railroad was called a station. Someone helped Harriet at each station.
Stay quiet and try not to move.
Is it safe to come out?
No. You must wait here a few more days.

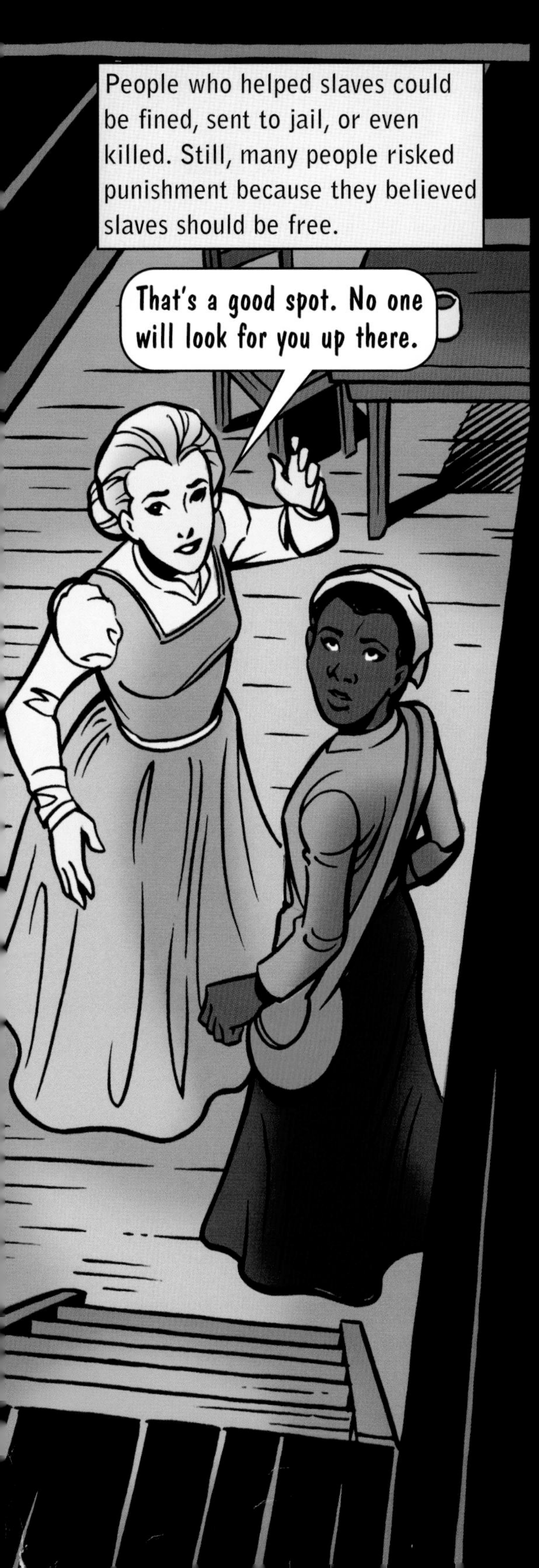
People who helped slaves could be fined, sent to jail, or even killed. Still, many people risked punishment because they believed slaves should be free.
That's a good spot. No one will look for you up there.
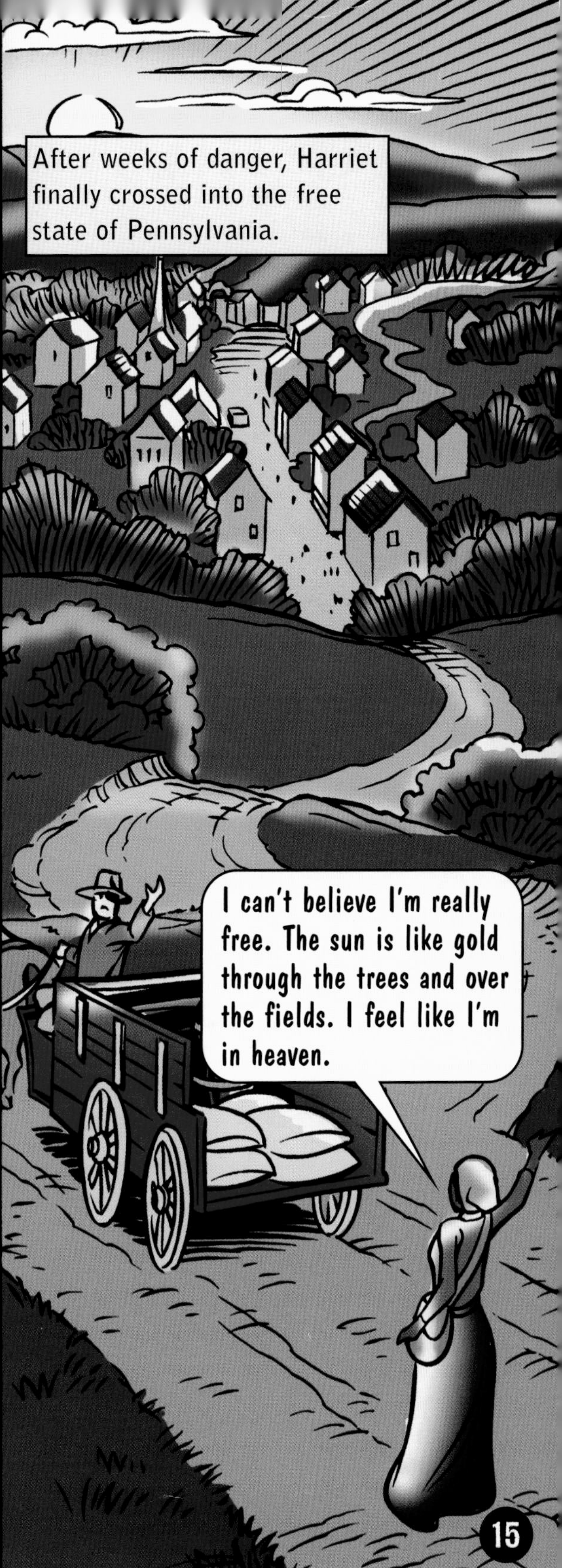
After weeks of danger, Harriet finally crossed into the free state of Pennsylvania.
I can't believe I'm really free. The sun is like gold through the trees and over the fields. I feel like I'm in heaven.

Chapter 3
The First Rescue

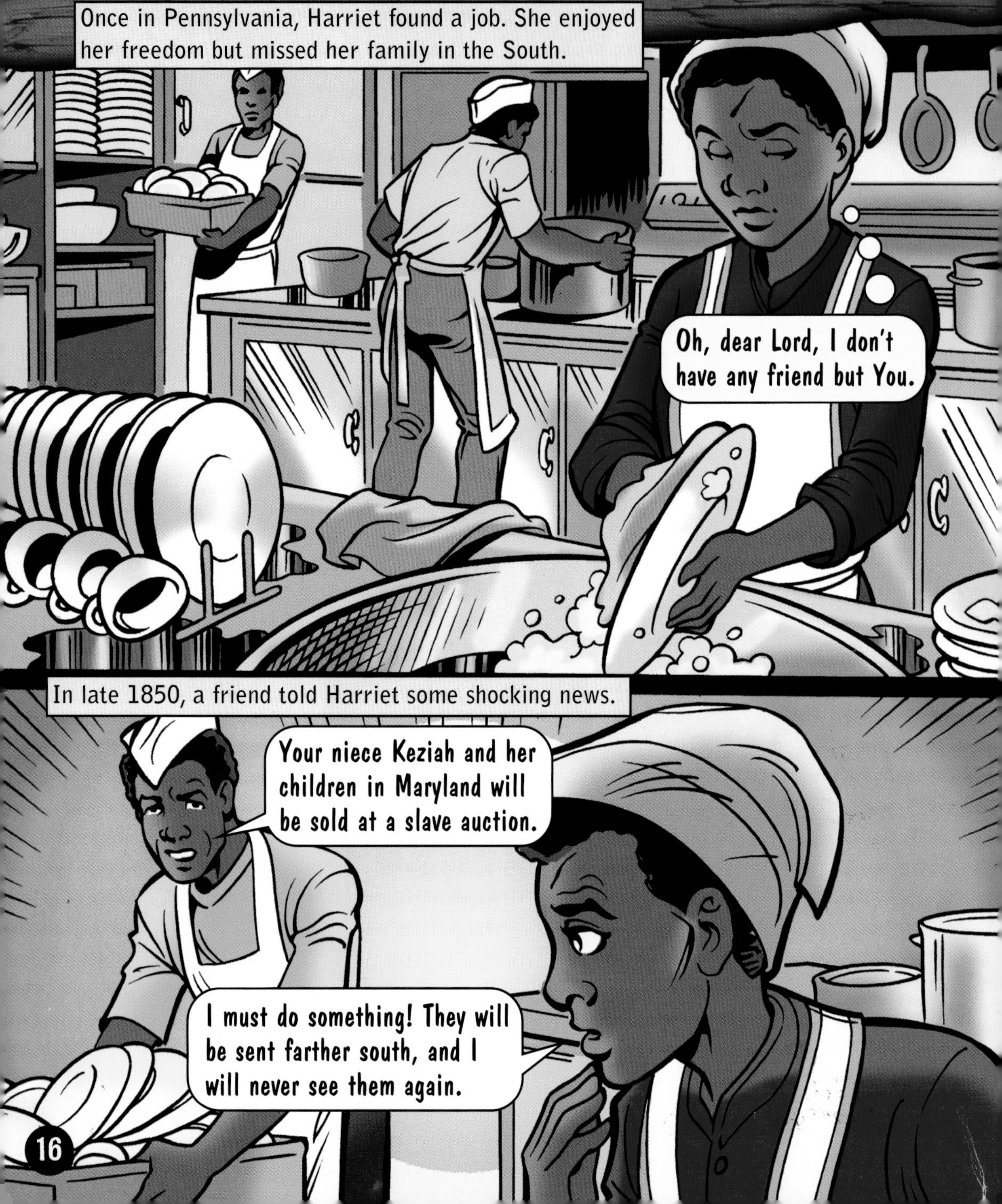
Once in Pennsylvania, Harriet found a job. She enjoyed her freedom but missed her family in the South.
Oh, dear Lord, I don't have any friend but You.
In late 1850, a friend told Harriet some shocking news.
Your niece Keziah and her children in Maryland will be sold at a slave auction.
I must do something! They will be sent farther south, and I will never see them again.

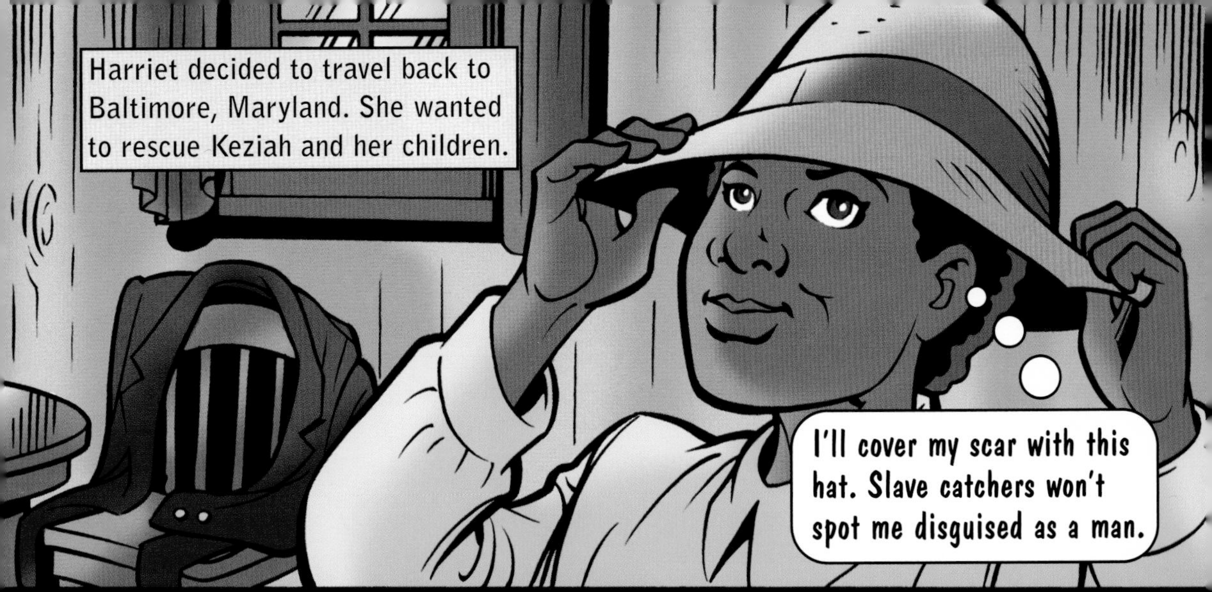
Harriet decided to travel back to Baltimore, Maryland. She wanted to rescue Keziah and her children.
I'll cover my scar with this hat. Slave catchers won't spot me disguised as a man.

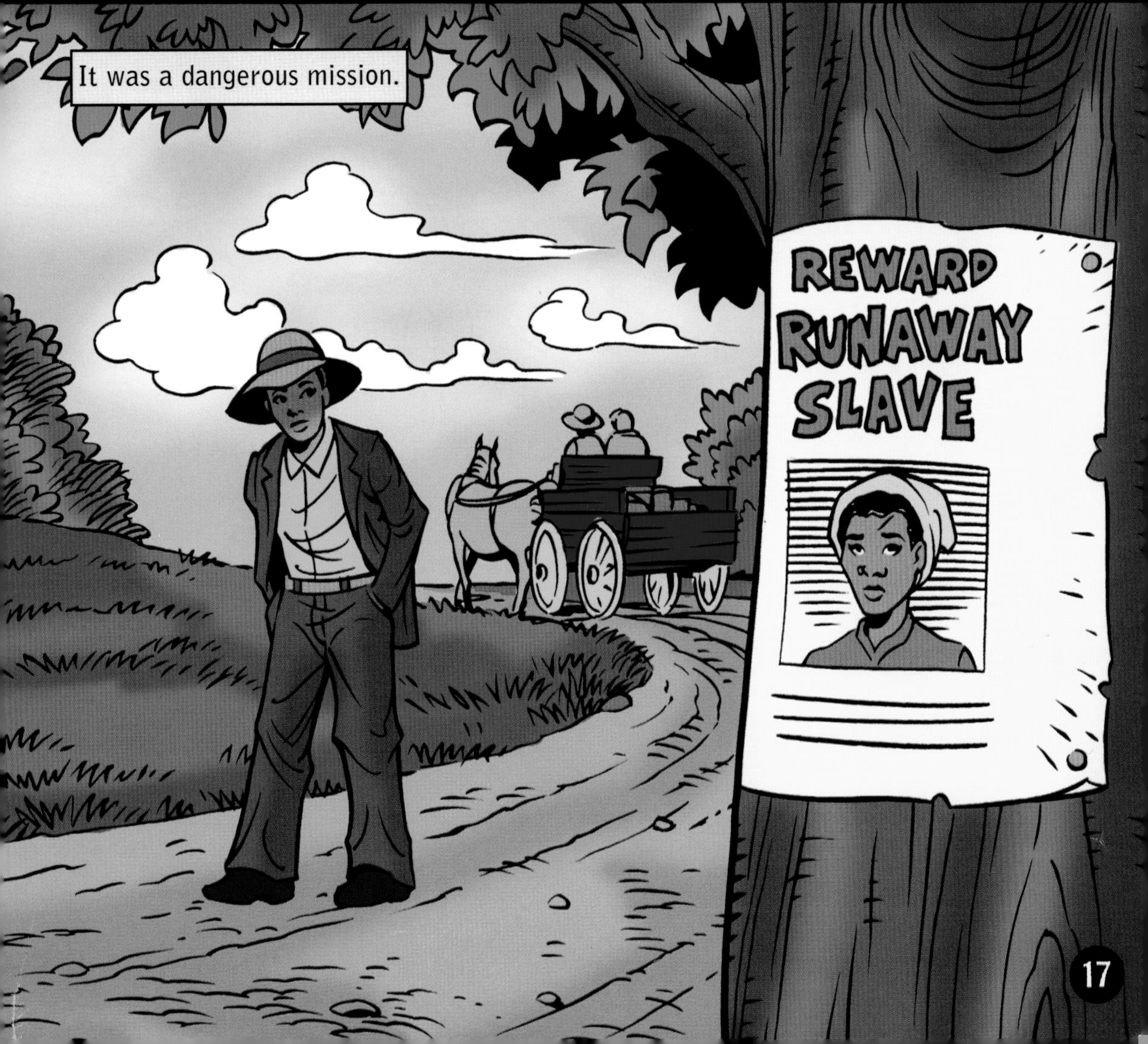
It was a dangerous mission.
REWARD
RUNAWAY SLAVE

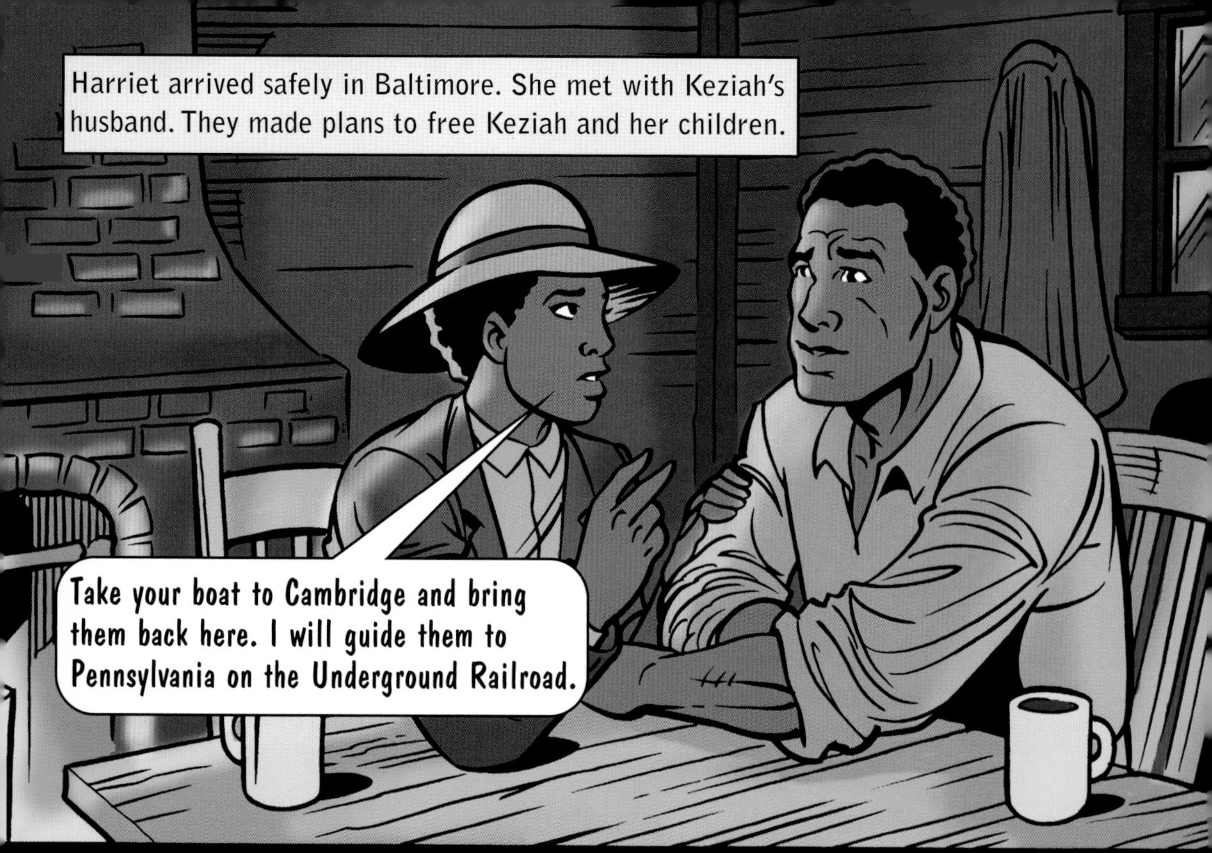
Harriet arrived safely in Baltimore. She met with Keziah's husband. They made plans to free Keziah and her children.
Take your boat to Cambridge and bring them back here. I will guide them to Pennsylvania on the Underground Railroad.

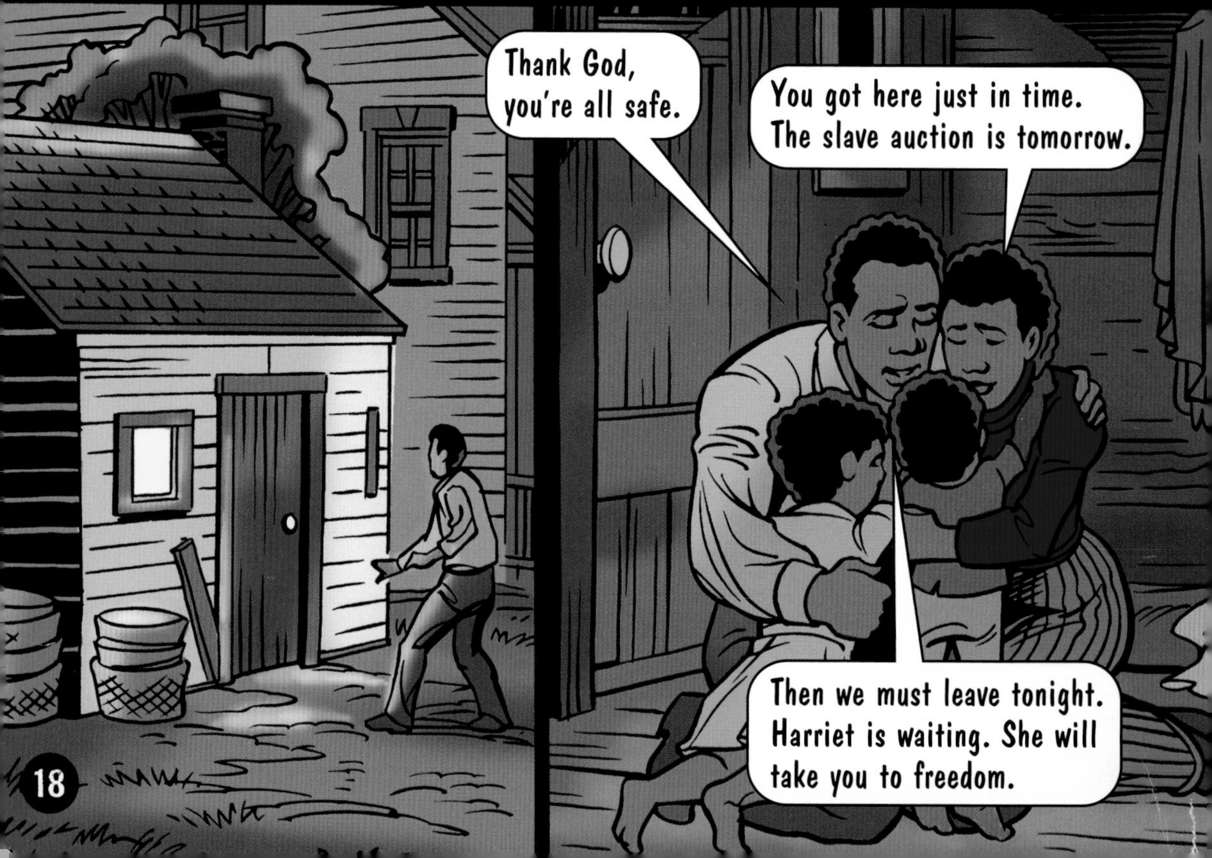
Thank God, you're all safe.
You got here just in time. The slave auction is tomorrow.
Then we must leave tonight. Harriet is waiting. She will take you to freedom.

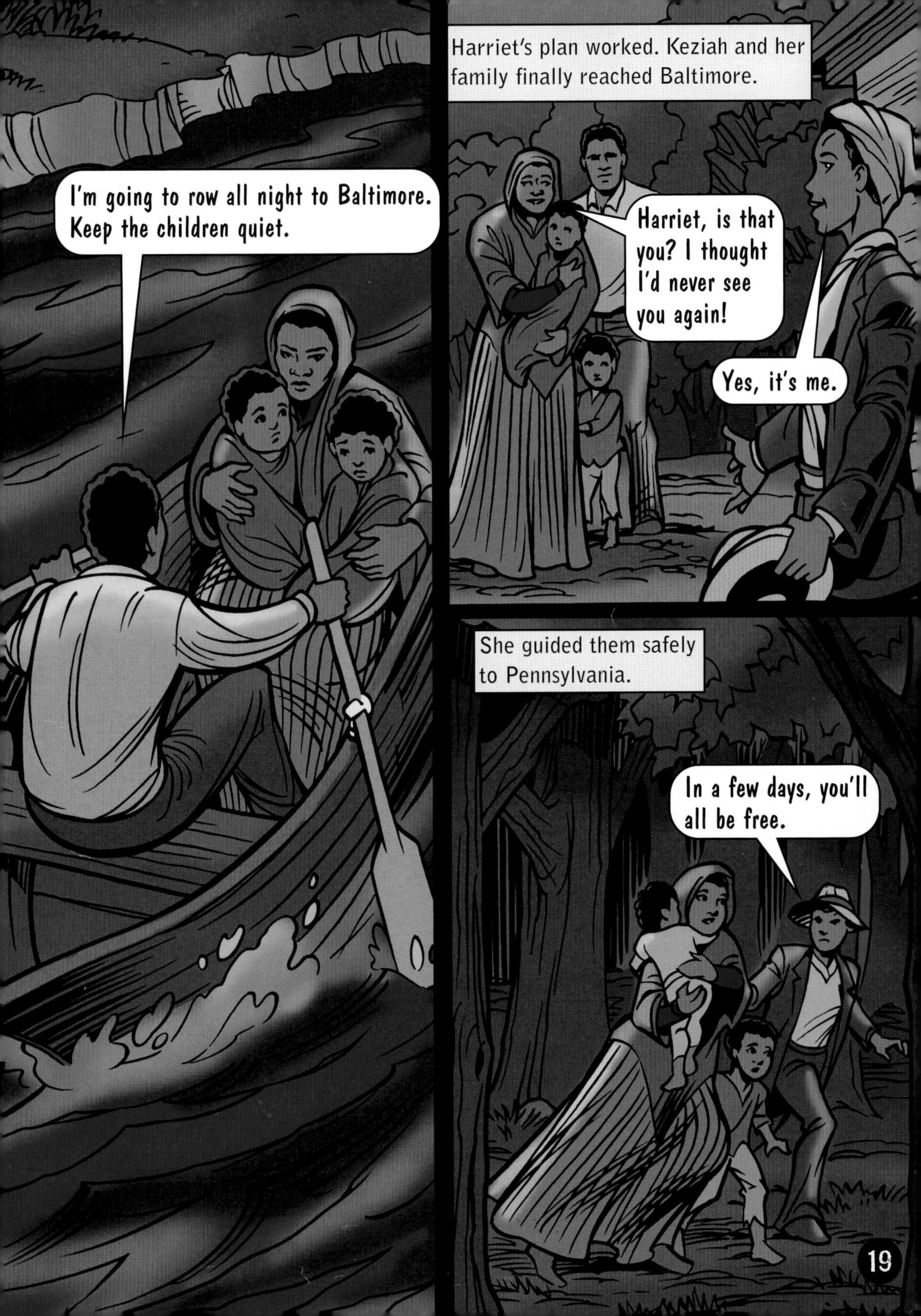
I'm going to row all night to Baltimore. Keep the children quiet.
Harriet's plan worked. Keziah and her family finally reached Baltimore.
Harriet, is that you? I thought I'd never see you again!
Yes, it's me.
She guided them safely to Pennsylvania.
In a few days, you'll all be free.

Chapter 4
Conductor on the Railroad

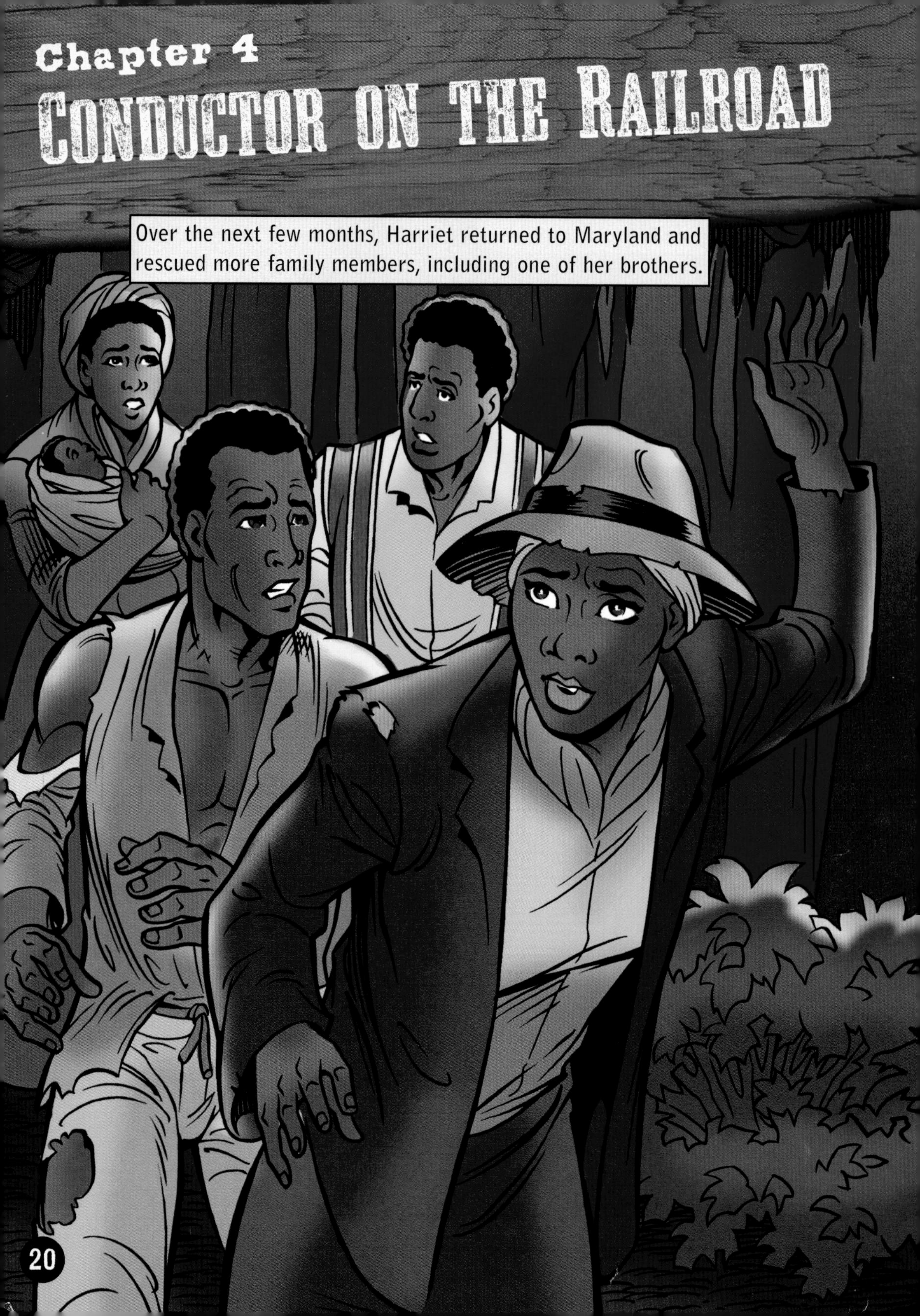
Over the next few months, Harriet returned to Maryland and rescued more family members, including one of her brothers.

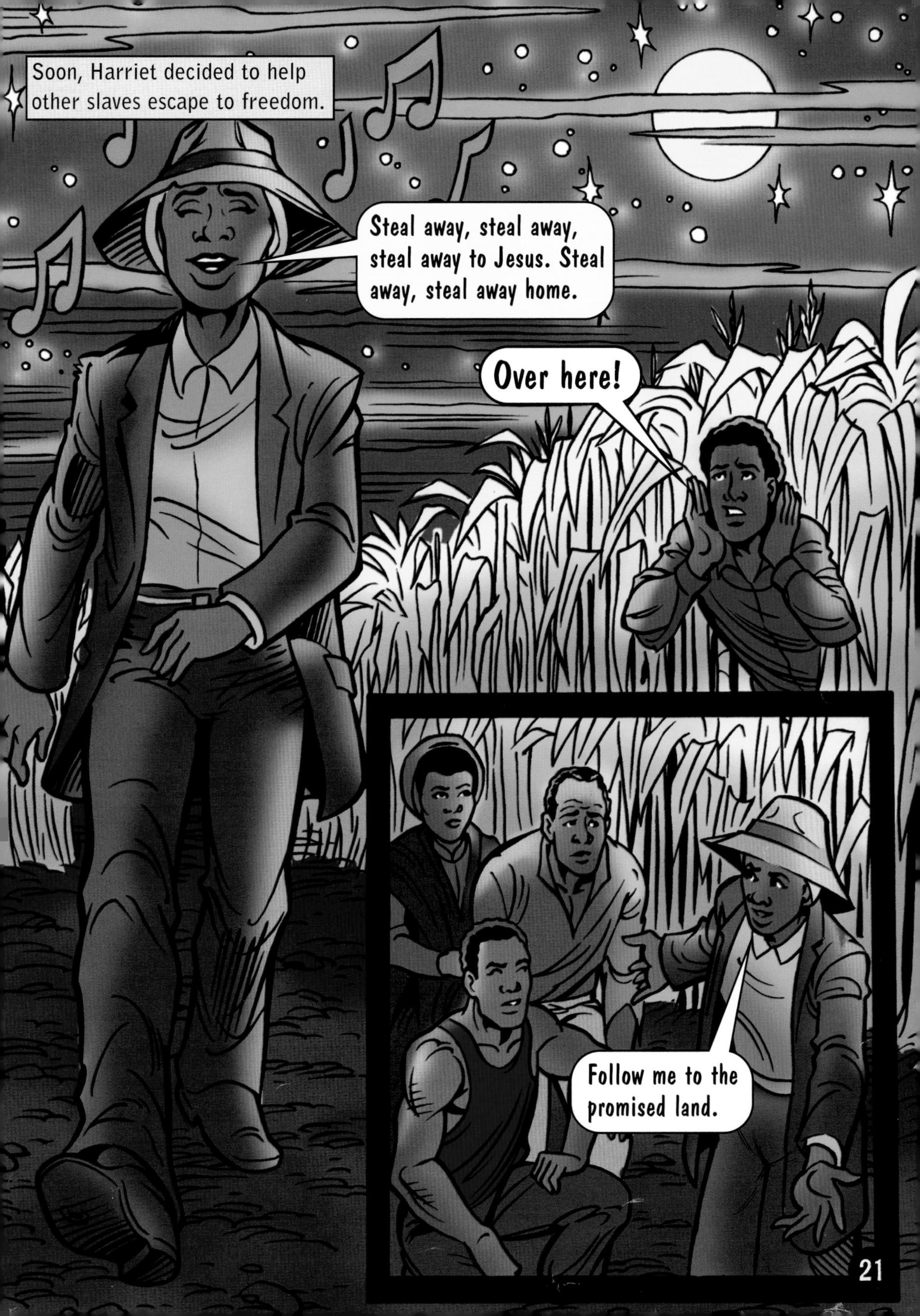
Soon, Harriet decided to help other slaves escape to freedom.
Steal away, steal away, steal away to Jesus. Steal away, steal away home.
Over here!
Follow me to the promised land.

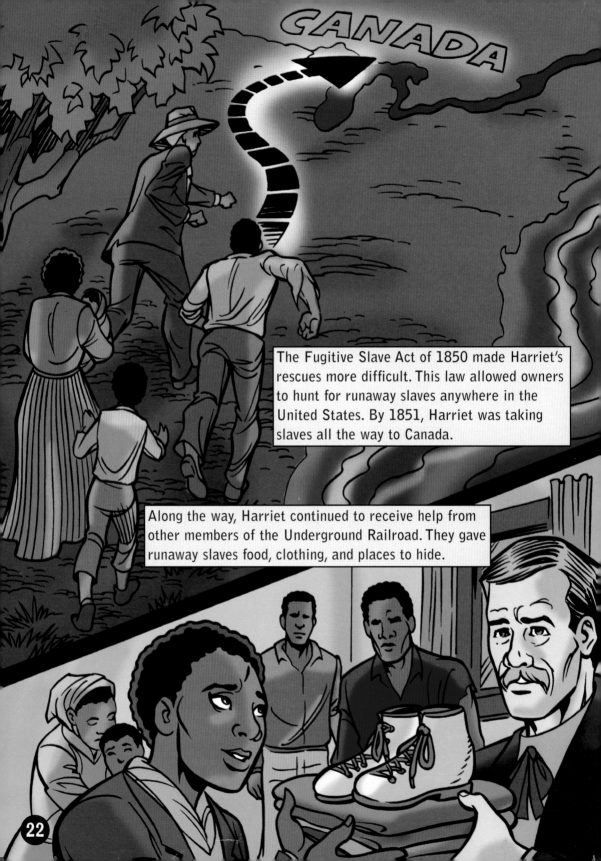

CANADA

The Fugitive Slave Act of 1850 made Harriet's rescues more difficult. This law allowed owners to hunt for runaway slaves anywhere in the United States. By 1851, Harriet was taking slaves all the way to Canada.

Along the way, Harriet continued to receive help from other members of the Underground Railroad. They gave runaway slaves food, clothing, and places to hide.

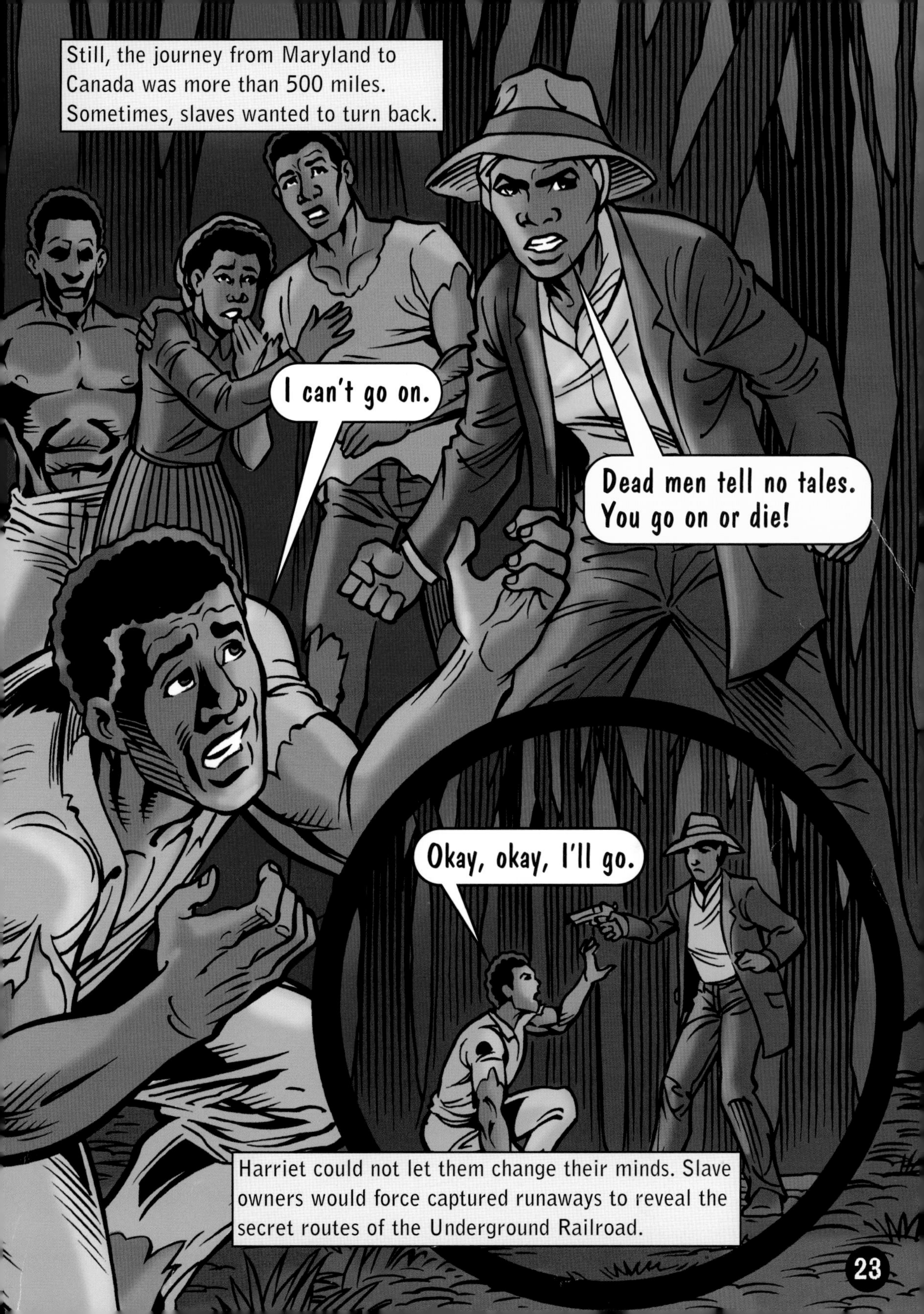

Still, the journey from Maryland to Canada was more than 500 miles. Sometimes, slaves wanted to turn back.
I can't go on.
Dead men tell no tales. You go on or die!
Okay, okay, I'll go.
Harriet could not let them change their minds. Slave owners would force captured runaways to reveal the secret routes of the Underground Railroad.

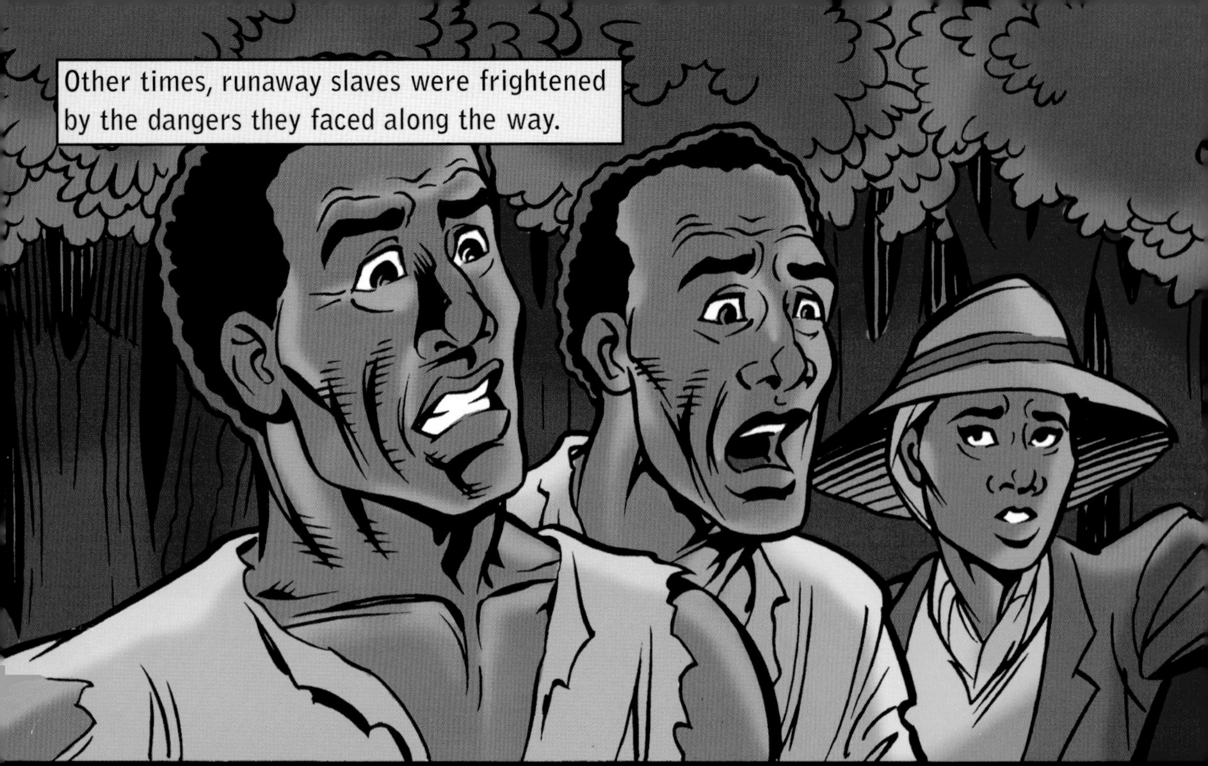
Other times, runaway slaves were frightened by the dangers they faced along the way.

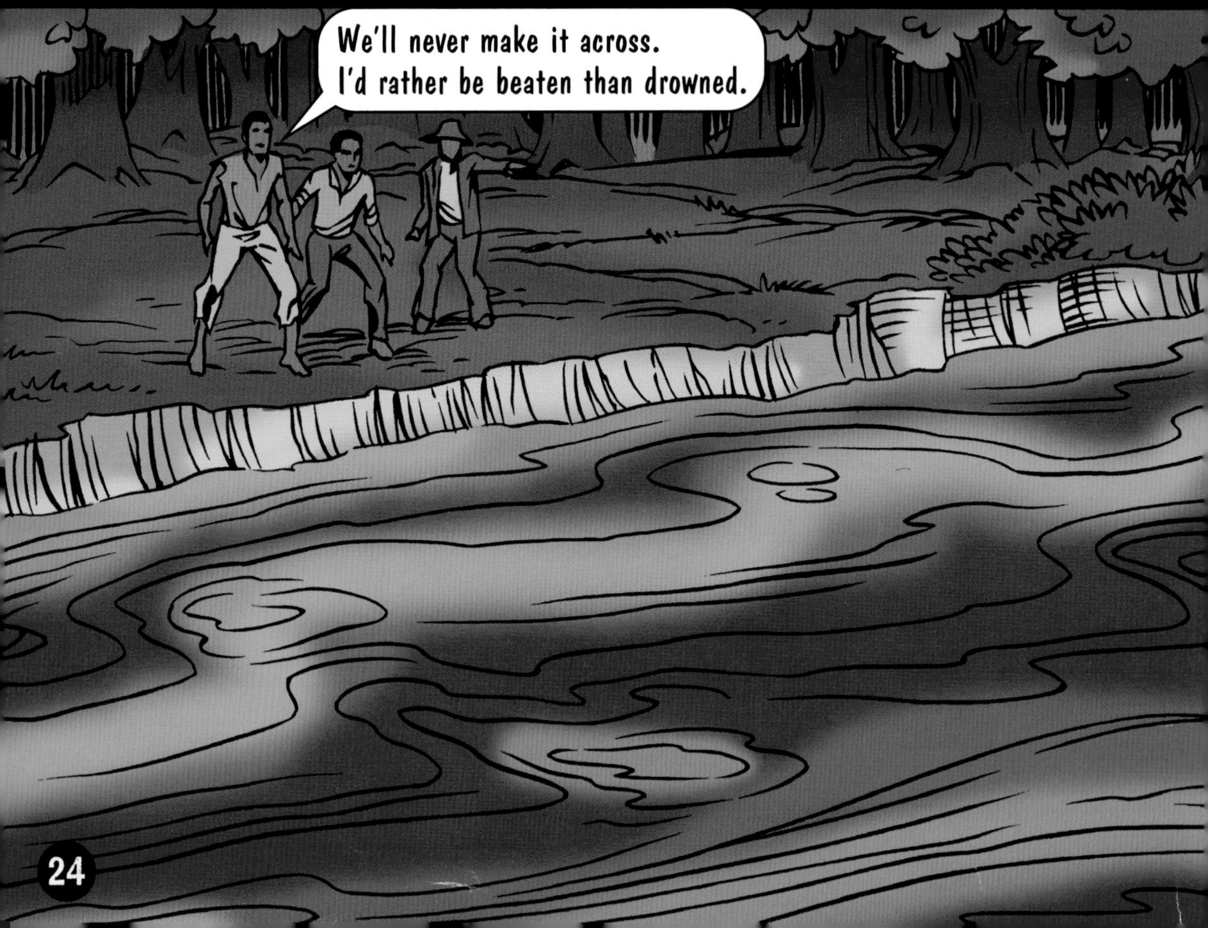
We'll never make it across. I'd rather be beaten than drowned.

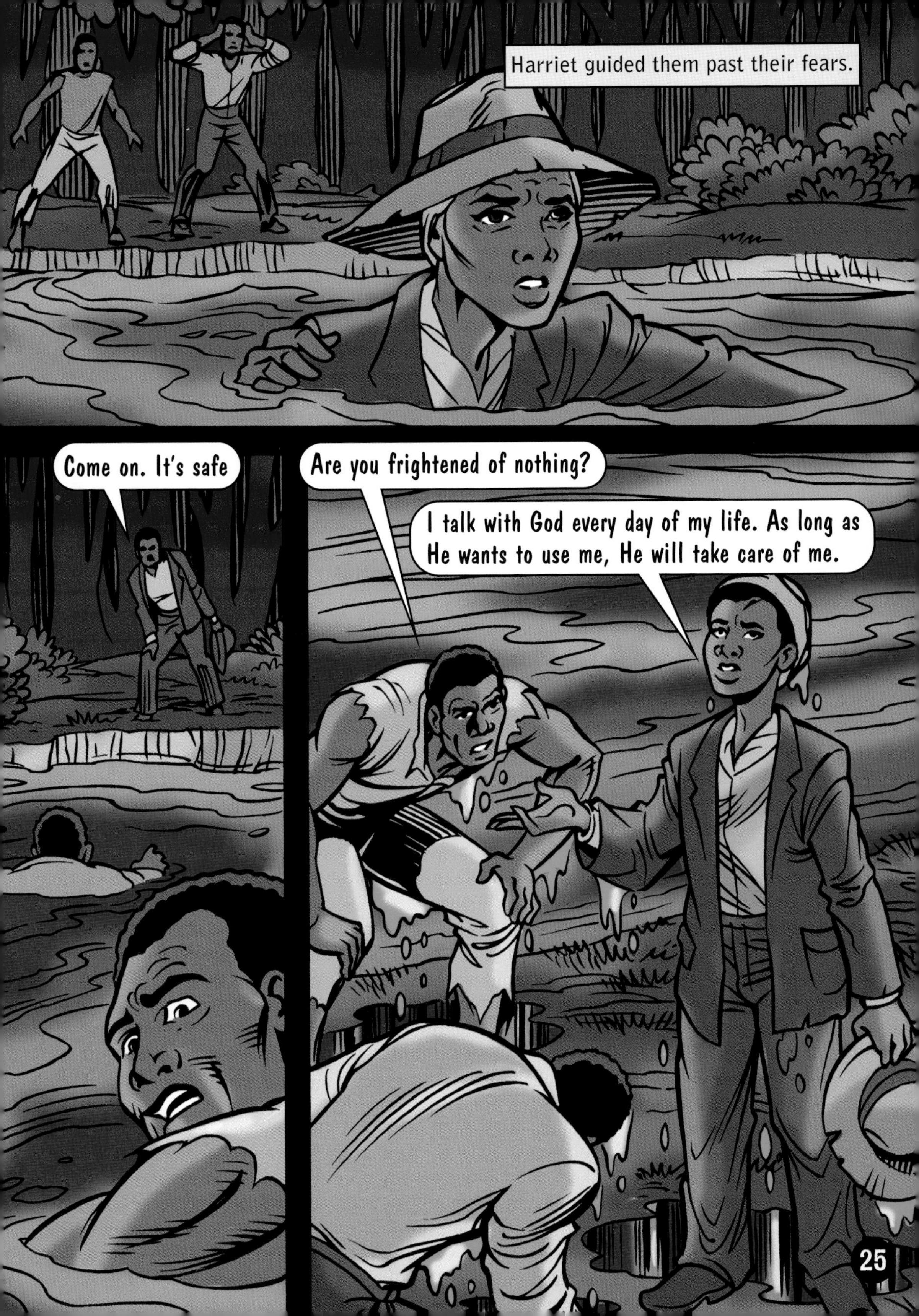

Harriet guided them past their fears.
Come on. It's safe
Are you frightened of nothing?
I talk with God every day of my life. As long as He wants to use me, He will take care of me.

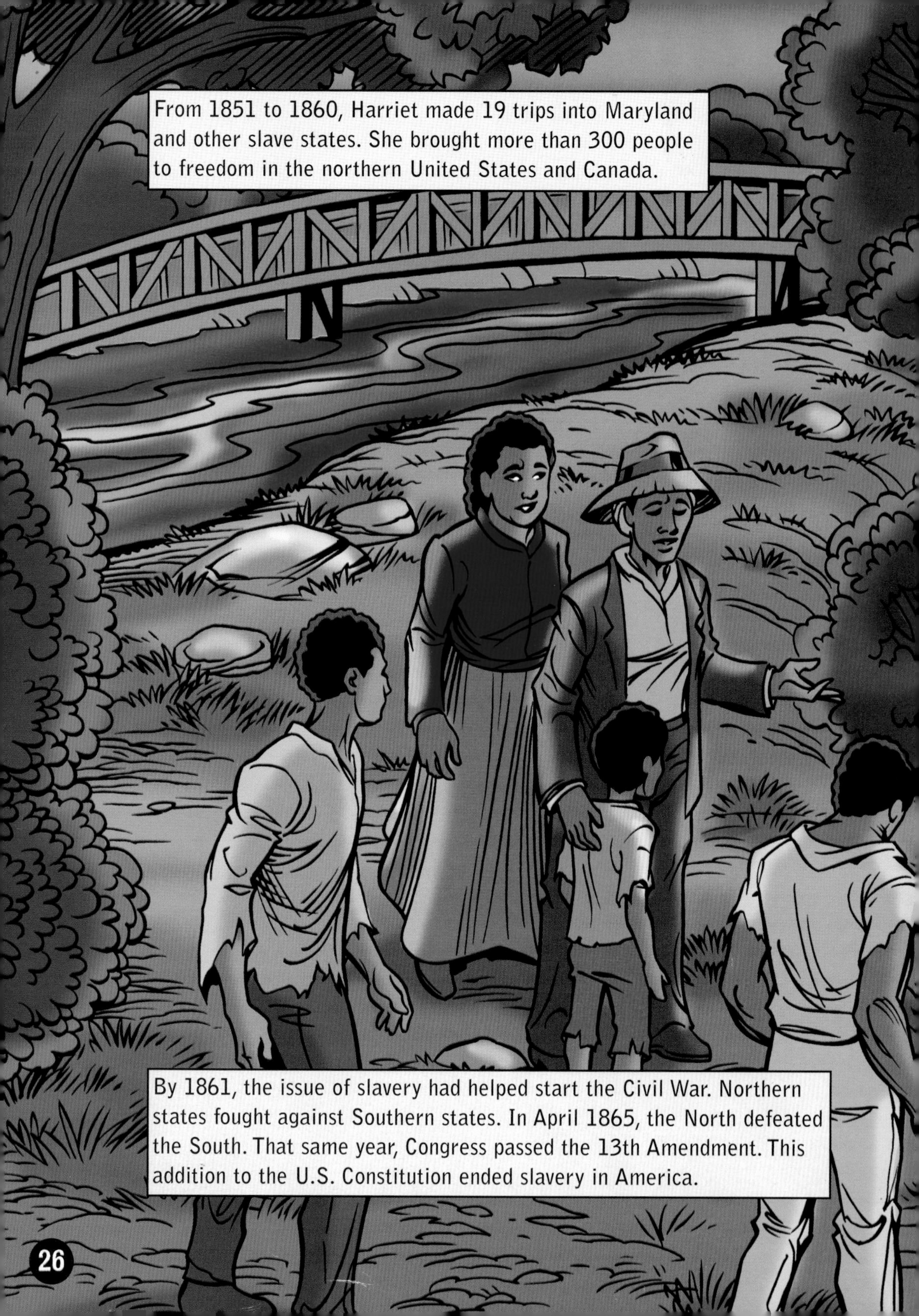
From 1851 to 1860, Harriet made 19 trips into Maryland and other slave states. She brought more than 300 people to freedom in the northern United States and Canada.
By 1861, the issue of slavery had helped start the Civil War. Northern states fought against Southern states. In April 1865, the North defeated the South. That same year, Congress passed the 13th Amendment. This addition to the U.S. Constitution ended slavery in America.

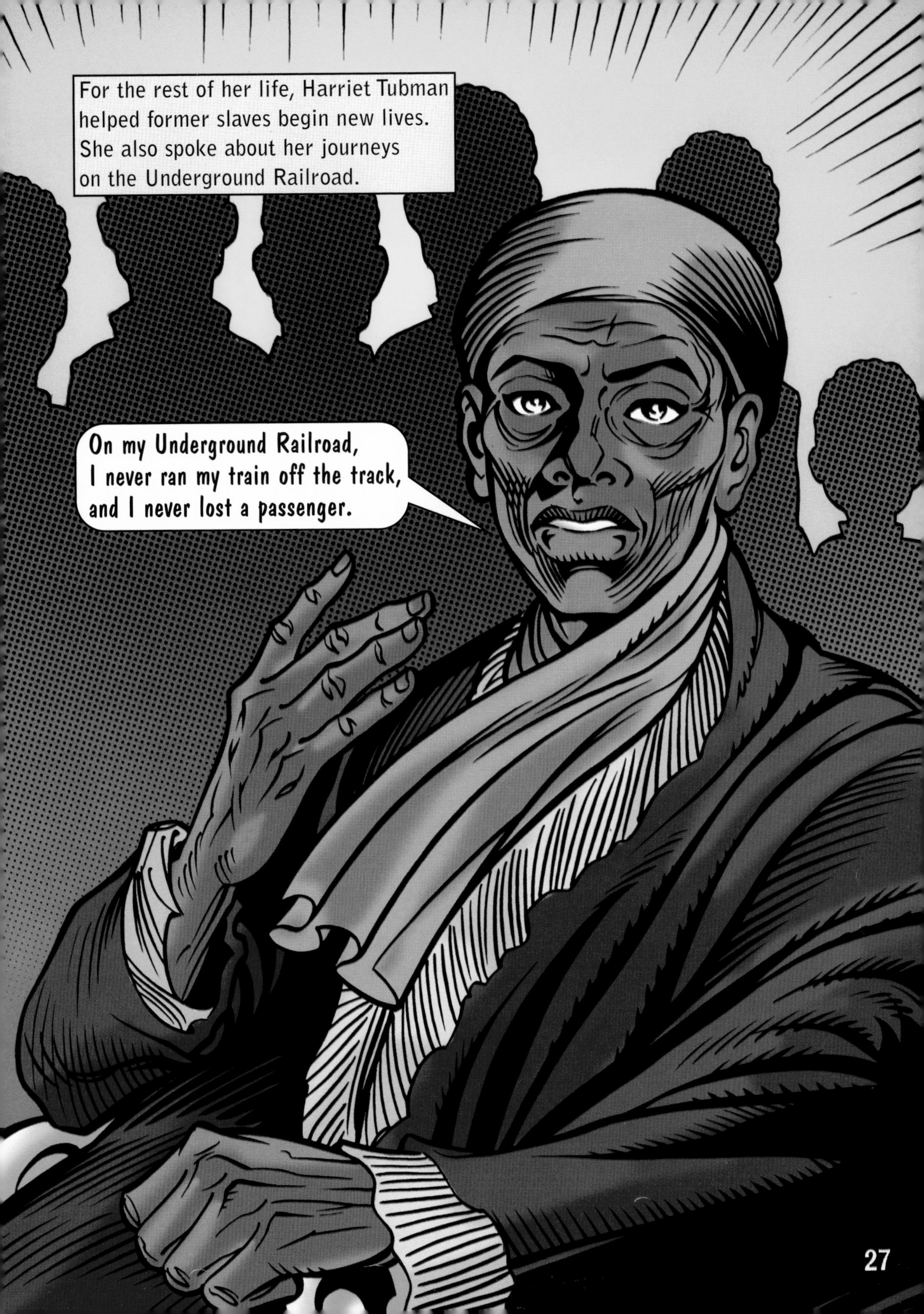
For the rest of her life, Harriet Tubman helped former slaves begin new lives. She also spoke about her journeys on the Underground Railroad.
On my Underground Railroad, I never ran my train off the track, and I never lost a passenger.

MORE ABOUT HARRIET TUBMAN

- At birth, Harriet Tubman was named Araminta Ross. Later, Harriet honored her family by taking her mother's first name.

- After her head injury, Harriet would faint or fall asleep several times a day. Harriet said she experienced visions of the future during many of these "spells." Some people believe that Harriet's visions helped her avoid being captured.

- Harriet used songs to send secret messages. Sometimes the songs warned runaway slaves of danger ahead. Harriet often sang "Wade in the Water" when slave catchers and their dogs were approaching. This song signaled runaway slaves to get off the trail and into a river or swamp. Walking through water would help throw the dogs off their scent.

- In 1851, Harriet returned to the South to find her husband, John Tubman. She wanted John to come with her to the North. Unfortunately, John had married another woman and did not want to leave.

- Harriet rescued many of her family members from slavery in the South. In 1857, she brought her parents north to freedom in St. Catharines, Ontario, Canada.

During one rescue, Harriet had a bad toothache. Instead of suffering with the pain, Harriet knocked out two of her teeth with a pistol.

During the Civil War, Harriet became a nurse for the Union army in the North. Later, she helped the army as a spy and a scout.

In 1863, Harriet led 150 Union soldiers on a raid in South Carolina. The troops freed 750 slaves and destroyed enemy supplies.

After the Civil War ended, Harriet headed for Auburn, New York. While living in Auburn, she worked with women's rights groups, raised money for schools, and helped in her church.

On June 23, 1908, Harriet opened the Harriet Tubman Home. This charity shelter helped older and ill African Americans in New York.

On March 10, 1913, Harriet died at her home in Auburn, New York. Since 1953, the Harriet Tubman Home has been a memorial to Tubman's life.

GLOSSARY

blackout (BLAK-out)—a loss of vision or memory for a short period of time

Congress (KONG-griss)—the government body of the United States that makes laws

Constitution (kon-stuh-TOO-shuhn)—the written system of laws in the United States that states the rights of the people and powers of the government

overseer (OH-vur-see-uhr)—a person in charge of watching and punishing slaves

slavery (SLAY-vur-ee)—the owning of other people; slaves are forced to work without pay.

station (STAY-shuhn)—a hiding place on the Underground Railroad

INTERNET SITES

FactHound offers a safe, fun way to find Internet sites related to this book. All of the sites on FactHound have been researched by our staff.

Here's how:

1. Visit *www.facthound.com*
2. Type in this special code **0736838295** for age-appropriate sites. Or enter a search word related to this book for a more general search.
3. Click on the **Fetch It** button.

FactHound will fetch the best sites for you!

READ MORE

Healy, Nick. *Harriet Tubman: Conductor to Freedom.* Fact Finders Biographies. Mankato, Minn.: Capstone Press, 2005.

Klingel, Cynthia Fitterer. *Harriet Tubman: Abolitionist and Underground Railroad Conductor.* Our People. Chanhassen, Minn.: Child's World, 2004.

Monroe, Judy. *The Underground Railroad: Bringing Slaves North to Freedom.* Let Freedom Ring. Mankato, Minn.: Bridgestone Books, 2003.

BIBLIOGRAPHY

Bradford, Sarah H. *Harriet Tubman: The Moses of Her People.* Bedford, Mass.: Applewood Books, 1993. A facsimile of *Scenes in the Life of Harriet Tubman.* Auburn, N.Y.: W.J. Moses, 1869.

Clinton, Catherine. *Harriet Tubman: The Road to Freedom.* Boston: Little, Brown, 2004.

Conrad, Earl. *Harriet Tubman.* Washington, D.C.: The Associated Publishers, 1943.

Humez, Jean McMahon. *Harriet Tubman: The Life and the Life Stories.* Madison, Wis.: University of Wisconsin Press, 2003.

Johnson, Weldon James, and J. Rosamond Johnson, comp. *The Books of American Negro Spirituals.* New York: Viking Press, 1940.

Larson, Kate Clifford. *Bound for the Promised Land: Harriet Tubman: Portrait of an American Hero.* New York: Random House, 2005.

INDEX

Calderstone Middle School
160 Calderstone Rd.
Brampton, ON
L6P 2L7